HOW DO YOU WISH Jesus A HAPPY BIRTHDAY?

Kason, I am so grateful for how you always say yes to my big dreams and ideas!
Thank you for always supporting me!

For Kerrington, may you always look for ways to shine the Light of Jesus on those around you.

I love the memory of you helping me find the right words to bring this story to life!

WRITTEN BY TAMARA MENGES

ILLUSTRATIONS BY EMILY SPIKINGS

How do you wish Jesus a happy birthday?

How do I give gifts to Jesus my friend?
Is there a gift or a card I can send?

Read the Bible to discover
a whole bunch of clues
of how kindness to others
is a gift for Him too!

Do you go to the playground during the day?
Find a friend who looks lonely and ask them to play.

I bet cookies are loved by all your neighbors. When sprinkles are added, baking won't feel like labor.

First days are scary
for new kids at school.
Give a high-five
and help them feel cool.

Our first responders serve and protect. Bake them some cupcakes they'll never forget.

Is there a kid at your school with not much for lunch? Pack some extra to share—something yummy to munch.

Our country stays safe
thanks to brave men and women.
Craft and send special cards
to brighten their season.

Kids in a hospital
surely feel blue.
Books, toys, and cards
could bring a smile or two.

Not every kid gets
new toys for Christmas.
Buy some to donate
and share God's goodness.

A shoebox of gifts
filled to the brim
shared across the globe
glorifies Him.

Throw a party for Jesus
His love can't be beat.
A yummy treat for all
makes a birthday complete!

Wishing Jesus a happy Birthday
can be done many ways,
when you show kindness to others
through each of your days.

How Do You Wish Jesus a Happy Birthday?
was inspired by Matthew 25:34-40.

"Then the King will say to those on his right, 'Come, you who are blessed by my Father; take your inheritance, the kingdom prepared for you since the creation of the world.
For I was hungry and you gave me something to eat,
I was thirsty and you gave me something to drink,
I was a stranger and you invited me in,
I needed clothes and you clothed me, I was sick and you looked after me,
I was in prison and you came to visit me.'
"Then the righteous will answer him, 'Lord, when did we see you hungry and feed you, or thirsty and give you something to drink?
When did we see you a stranger and invite you in,
or needing clothes and clothe you?
When did we see you sick or in prison and go to visit you?'
"The King will reply, 'Truly I tell you, whatever you did for one of the least of these brothers and sisters of mine, you did for me.'"

Every time we put someone else first, every time we show kindness, or pay attention to the needs of others. And even when we simply say, "thank you" or show gratitude we share Jesus. We shine His light that is within us, and in doing so we wish Him a, "happy birthday!"

Merry Christmas and Happy Birthday Jesus!

In Him,
Tamara

HOW DO YOU WISH Jesus A HAPPY BIRTHDAY?

SCAN ME

Written and published for
Light Filled Home
www.Lightfilledhome.com